Glorious
Layered Desserts

GLORY ALBIN

Photography by Gene Chutka

FRONT TABLE BOOKS
AN IMPRINT OF CEDAR FORT, INC.
SPRINGVILLE, UTAH

© 2014 Glory Albin
Photography © 2014 Gene Chutka
All rights reserved.

ISBN 13: 978-1-4621-1913-4

Published by Front Table Books, an imprint of Cedar Fort, Inc.
2373 W. 700 S., Springville, UT 84663
Distributed by Cedar Fort, Inc., www.cedarfort.com

Library of Congress Cataloging-in-Publication Data on file

Cover and page design by Erica Dixon
Cover design © 2014 by Lyle Mortimer
Edited by Casey J. Winters

Printed in China

10 9 8 7 6 5 4 3 2 1

CONTENTS

INTRODUCTION

*Want to know the secret to creating beautiful,
delicious desserts your friends and family will love? It's all about layers!*

Glorious Layered Desserts gives you a recipe collection of delicious dessert components and then shows you how to creatively layer different flavors and textures to create unforgettable desserts!

Whether you need a treat you can make ahead, something quick and easy, or an impressive dessert for a special occasion, *Glorious Layered Desserts* has the perfect treat for you!

In the first half of the book you'll find dozens of beautiful, creative, and mouthwatering layered desserts.

These recipes are made using two or more delicious dessert components, layered in a variety of beautiful ways.

With many of these recipes, you'll find tips on how to save time, how to adjust the recipe to your tastes, and even more creative recipe ideas.

The second half of the book contains all the essential recipes needed to create each incredible layered dessert. These are recipes you'll be able to rely on again and again to create delicious desserts.

EQUIPMENT & TECHNIQUES

*Having the right tools for the job will make any
kitchen task more enjoyable—and more successful.*

Electric mixer: Many of the recipes in this book will require the use of either a large stand mixer (preferred) or a handheld electric mixer. I have used a large (KitchenAid) stand mixer in any recipes where whipping is listed. Using a handheld mixer will take longer but will produce almost identical results.

Handheld whisk: Use a whisk in any recipe that requires stirring but does not require an electric mixer (such as pudding, chocolate sauce, and caramel sauce).

Spatula: Rubber spatulas are the perfect tool to fold together ingredients. When the directions say "fold together," that means to incorporate two mixtures gently without deflating the air (that was added during whipping). Run the spatula down one side of the bowl and then up through the center, repeating until the two mixtures are combined.

Piping bag and tips: For many of the layered desserts, you will get the most perfect layers by piping the ingredients into the glass or dish. I like using a large (sixteen-inch) reusable piping bag, fitted with a coupler and large tips. To easily fill the piping bag, place the bag in a large glass (after you have added the coupler and tip), fold down the top of the bag, and then use a large spoon or spatula to fill the bag two-thirds to three-fourths full. Once filled, pull up the edges of the bag and twist the bag just above where the ingredients are. Hold the twist closed with your thumb against your hand and then use your fingers to press on the bag, and squeeze out the contents. (See additional resources, page 132, for piping bags and tips.)

Piping bag alternative: If you do not have a large piping bag, you can use a gallon-size ziplock-type plastic bag to pipe the various layers into your dishes. Put the plastic bag in a large glass (just as you would the piping bag), fold down the top, and fill the bag two-thirds full. Pull up the bag and seal it closed. Snip off one corner of the bag and squeeze contents into your dishes, as desired.

ADDITIONAL TIPS FOR SUCCESS

A standard dessert serving is ½–¾ cup (4–6 oz.). Keep this in mind as you plan how many desserts you want to make. If you are using large glasses (8–10 oz.), you will be able to make fewer desserts than the listed range. If you are using mini, taster-sized glasses (2–3 oz.), you will be able to make more than the listed range.

Read the whole recipe. Depending on the recipe, you may need to consider the chilling or baking time before you start the recipe. Make sure you have all the necessary ingredients on hand as well.

TIME-SAVING OPTIONS

As much as I love the process of making elaborate desserts, I know the importance of having recipes I can turn to when I'm short on time. The desserts below are quick and easy but will still produce a beautiful and delicious treat.

*Many of the individual dessert components ("Essential Recipes")
can be made in advance to save time on the day of serving.*

MAKE IN ADVANCE

1 full day

Creamy No-Bake Cheesecake	p. 108
Stabilized Whipped Cream	p. 126
Homemade Fruit Sauce	p. 122
Vanilla Panna Cotta	p. 111

Up to 2 days

Fudge Brownies	p. 87
Vanilla Sponge Cake	p. 95
Pumpkin Spice Cake	p. 91
Vanilla Pastry Cream	p. 115
Coconut Cream Pudding	p. 99
Chocolate Pudding	p. 105

1 week or more

Any crust/crumble	pp. 83–88
Caramel Sauce	p. 118
Chocolate Fudge Sauce	p. 121
Lemon Curd	p. 125
Sugared Nuts	p. 92

INGREDIENTS

Using quality ingredients is essential to creating delicious food. Choosing the correct ingredients will have a huge impact on the final results of your dish.

Butter: Chose high-quality full-fat butter. Margarine or reduced-fat butters have added water or other ingredients that will affect the results of your dish. The general standard in baking is to use unsalted butter. For the recipes in this book, using salted butter will also work, but be sure to reduce or eliminate any additional salt listed in the recipe.

Chocolate: The overall flavor of your finished product will be greatly affected by the quality of chocolate you use, so choose the best-quality chocolate available (in most cases, price and quality are directly related).

Cocoa powder: Use unsweetened cocoa powder, not a sweet cocoa or chocolate mix, in the recipes in this book. As with any chocolate, using the best-quality cocoa you can find will greatly affect the end results of your recipe. Choose rich, dark, flavorful cocoa powders.

Cream: When heavy cream is listed in a recipe, make sure you are using heavy cream, not half-and-half. Heavy cream is sometimes labeled "heavy whipping cream," and it is usually 36 percent milk fat.

Cream cheese: Choose high-quality full-fat cream cheese. Reduced-fat cream cheese contains extra water and will affect the results of the recipe. In any recipe that calls for cream cheese, you should beat the cream cheese until smooth before adding any other ingredients. If there are lumps in the cream cheese when you add other ingredients to the mixer, creating a smooth dessert will be nearly impossible.

Lemon and lime (zest and juice): In recipes that call for citrus juice or zest, use fresh juice (not bottled juice) and fresh zest (not dried). Fresh juice and zest have much more flavor and will produce tastier results.

Milk: In recipes that call for milk, use whole or 2 percent milk. If you only have non-fat or 1 percent milk, add a little cream or half-and-half. A few recipes in this book that require milk will say "any fat content;" in these cases, feel free to use any milk you have on hand.

Vanilla: When vanilla extract (or vanilla) is listed in a recipe, use good-quality pure vanilla extract, not imitation vanilla. Vanilla bean paste is usually sold near vanilla extract and may be used in place of, or in addition to, vanilla extract. Using vanilla bean paste in a recipe will result in visible flecks of vanilla beans in the finished recipe.

Layered Desserts

APPLE CRISP

Makes 6-7 servings

Total Time: 30 minutes

FROM START TO FINISH

This classic dessert is perfect for fall, but it's so delicious you will want to make it all year round!

Dessert Components

Oatmeal Nut Crumble
(see page 88)

Cinnamon Apples
(see below)

½ recipe Whipped Cream
(see page 126)
or vanilla ice cream

Assembly

1. Prepare oatmeal nut crumble. Bake and cool.

2. While the crumble bakes, prepare cinnamon apples using recipe below.

3. Make whipped cream (or use canned whipped cream or vanilla ice cream).

4. When all your components are prepared, add a generous layer of oatmeal nut crumble (2–3 tablespoons) to the bottom of each dish. Top with a layer of cinnamon apples.

5. Garnish with whipped cream and a bit of oatmeal nut crumble just before serving. This dessert can be enjoyed warm or cool.

CINNAMON APPLES

Ingredients

3 medium tart, firm apples
(such as Granny Smith)

3 Tbsp. brown sugar

¼ cup butter

½ tsp. cinnamon

Directions

Peel apples and dice into small pieces (about ½-inch cubes). Add apples, brown sugar, butter, and cinnamon to a skillet and cook over medium-high heat. Cook until the apples begin to soften but still have some texture (4–5 minutes). Remove from heat and cool a bit before assembling dessert. The apples can be made ahead of time (up to 1 day) and layered in the dessert cold or reheated before serving.

BANANA CARAMEL CREAM DESSERT

Makes 6-8 servings

Total Time: 4 hours

PREP: 30 minutes

COOLING: 3+ hours

ASSEMBLY: 20 minutes

The classic flavors of banana cream pie are dressed up with the addition of rich caramel. These simple flavors combine to create a surprisingly delicious treat.

Dessert Components

Vanilla Pastry Cream
(see page 115)

Caramel Sauce
(see page 118)

Graham Cracker Crumble
(see page 84)

Whipped Cream
(see page 126)

3–4 large ripe bananas

Assembly

1. Make vanilla pastry cream and chill as directed (about 3 hours).

2. Make caramel sauce and cool (at least 1 hour).

3. Prepare graham cracker crumble. Cool and set aside.

4. Make whipped cream, just before assembly.

5. Slice bananas, just before assembly.

6. Begin assembly by adding about 2 tablespoons graham cracker crumble to the bottom of each dish. Add a layer of vanilla pastry cream. Add 3–4 slices of banana. Drizzle a bit of caramel sauce on top of the bananas. Add a layer of whipped cream. Repeat the layers: crust (about 1 tablespoon), pastry cream, bananas, caramel, whipped cream.

7. Just before serving, top with a slice of banana, a few graham cracker crumbs, and a drizzle of caramel.

BANANA SPLIT CHEESECAKE

Makes 6-8 servings

Total Time: 3½ hours

PREP: 45 minutes

CHILLING: 3 hours

ASSEMBLY: 10 minutes

Creamy cheesecake gets an updated twist with all the flavors of a banana split.

Dessert Components

Graham Cracker Crumble
(see page 84)

Creamy Cheesecake
(see page 108),
with adjustments

Chocolate Fudge Sauce
(see page 121)
or good-quality
chocolate sauce

**1½ cups fresh
chopped strawberries**

2 tsp. sugar

½ recipe Whipped Cream
(see page 126),
or canned whipped cream

2-3 bananas

maraschino cherries

sprinkles (optional)

Assembly

1. Prepare graham cracker crumble. Bake and cool.

2. Prepare creamy cheesecake, but reduce the lemon juice to 2 tablespoons and add 3 tablespoons Greek yogurt or sour cream.

3. Add 2–3 tablespoons of graham cracker crumble to the bottom of each dessert dish. Use a small glass (such as a shot glass or glass spice bottle) to tap down the "crust" and then pour the creamy cheesecake on top of crust. Place in the refrigerator and chill for about 3 hours. The cheesecake can be made up to 1 day in advance.

4. If desired, while the cheesecake is chilling, make chocolate fudge sauce.

5. Shortly before serving, chop strawberries and top with sugar. Toss together and put in the refrigerator for about 15 minutes.

6. Make whipped cream. Then slice bananas.

7. Gather cheesecakes from refrigerator and top with sliced bananas, chopped strawberries, and whipped cream. Add a drizzle of chocolate sauce, a maraschino cherry, and sprinkles.

More Ideas • • • • • • • • • • • • • • •

Mix and match the toppings as desired. Feel free to add a layer of canned crushed pineapple or fresh chopped pineapple.

BROWNIE BOTTOM COCONUT CREAM DESSERT

Total Time: 4 hours

PREP: 45 minutes

COOLING: 3+ hours

ASSEMBLY: 20 minutes

Makes 6–8 servings

Rich chocolate brownie and creamy coconut pudding come together to create an elegant and delicious dessert.

Dessert Components

Coconut Cream Pudding
(see page 99)

Caramel Sauce
(see page 118)

Fudge Brownies
(see page 87*)

**about ¾ cup
sweetened coconut**

½ recipe Whipped Cream
(see page 126)

*You will have brownie left over.

Assembly

1. Prepare coconut cream pudding and cool as directed (about 4 hours).

2. Make caramel sauce, and cool (1 hour or more).

3. Prepare brownies, and cool fully (1 hour or more).

4. Toast coconut, and set aside. To toast coconut, spread sweetened coconut on a baking sheet and bake in a preheated oven at 350°F for 5–8 minutes. Stir coconut after 3 minutes, and check every minute or so after.

5. Prepare whipped cream (just before assembly).

6. Cut brownies into small cubes, or use a circle cookie cutter slightly smaller than your dish to cut a circle-shaped brownie. Place brownie in the bottom of your dessert dishes. Add a layer of coconut cream pudding on top of the brownie layer. Top pudding with whipped cream, toasted coconut, and a drizzle of caramel.

BROWNIE STRAWBERRY SHORTCAKE

Total Time: 1½ hours

PREP: 20 minutes

BAKING: 25 minutes

COOLING: 1 hour

ASSEMBLY: 15 minutes

Makes 5–6 servings

Simple ingredients can still create an impressive dessert! This chocolate version of classic strawberry shortcake is a perfect summer treat.

Dessert Components

Fudge Brownies
(see page 87*)

2 baskets/pints fresh strawberries**

1 Tbsp. sugar

Whipped Cream
(see page 126)

*You will have brownie left over.

**Feel free to use more strawberries if you want to make more servings.

Assembly

1. Make brownies and cool fully. The brownies can be made up to 2 days in advance.

2. While the brownies cool, wash the strawberries, remove stems, and cut into bite-size pieces. Put chopped strawberries in a large bowl and sprinkle sugar over the berries. Stir to combine, then place bowl in the fridge (at least 15 minutes).

3. Once the brownies are cool, cut about ⅓ of the pan of brownies into small cubes.

4. Make whipped cream.

5. Begin assembly by adding a layer of brownie into each dish. Top with a layer of whipped cream and then strawberries. Repeat layers: brownie, whipped cream, strawberries.

More Ideas

Make the more traditional version of this dessert using vanilla sponge cake (page 95) or store-bought angel food cake or vanilla pound cake in place of the brownies. Try this recipe with a combination of fresh strawberries and raspberries.

CARAMEL APPLE CHEESECAKE

Total Time: 1½ hours

· ·

FROM START TO FINISH

Makes 6–7 servings

This dessert is sweet and tart, creamy and crunchy, and is one of our family favorites. The variety of flavors and textures come together to create one amazing dessert!

Dessert Components

Caramel Sauce
(see page 118),
or choose a good-quality
caramel sauce

Oatmeal Nut Crumble
(see page 88)

Cinnamon Apples
(see page 11)

Cheesecake Mousse
(see page 101)

½ recipe Whipped Cream
(see page 126),
garnish

Assembly

1. Make caramel sauce and allow to cool.

2. Prepare oatmeal nut crumble, bake, and cool.

3. Prepare cinnamon apples and allow to cool.

4. Make cheesecake mousse and put in the refrigerator until ready to assemble dessert.

5. Prepare whipped cream (or use canned whipped cream).

6. Begin assembly by adding a layer of cheesecake mousse to the bottom of each dish. Add a layer of cinnamon apples and then a sprinkling of oatmeal crumble and a drizzle of caramel sauce. Repeat layers: cheesecake mousse, cinnamon apples, oatmeal crumble, caramel sauce. Finish dessert with a garnish of whipped cream, a few apples, and a drizzle of caramel.

7. Serve immediately or keep in the refrigerator until ready to serve. Best when enjoyed within 2 hours of assembly.

CARAMEL BROWNIE TRIFLE

Makes 4–5 servings

Layer upon layer of delicious ingredients creates a sweet, indulgent dessert that is always a hit!

Total Time: 3 hours

PREP: 45 minutes

COOLING: 2+ hours

ASSEMBLY: 20 minutes

Dessert Components

Chocolate Pudding
(see page 105)

Caramel Sauce
(see page 118)

Fudge Brownies
(see page 87*)

3–4 toffee candy bars
(such as Heath)

Whipped Cream
(see page 126)

You will have brownie left over.

Assembly

1. Prepare pudding and cool as directed (at least 2 hours).

2. Make caramel sauce and cool (at least 1 hour).

3. Prepare brownies, cool (at least 1 hour), and then cut into small cubes.

4. Crush candy bars by smashing wrapped bars with a rolling pin.

5. Make whipped cream, just before assembly.

6. Begin assembly by adding a layer of chocolate pudding to the bottom of each dish. Add a layer of brownie pieces. Top with whipped cream, and then sprinkle some toffee candy and add a drizzle of caramel. Repeat layers: pudding, brownie, whipped cream, toffee, caramel.

CHOCOLATE COCONUT LAYERED PUDDING

Total Time: 4 hours

PREP: 30 minutes

COOLING: 3+ hours

ASSEMBLY: 20 minutes

Makes 7–9 servings

The flavors of chocolate and coconut complement each other so well and look beautiful in this simple two-tone dessert.

Dessert Components

Coconut Cream Pudding
(see page 99*)

Chocolate Pudding
(see page 105)

¾ cup sweetened coconut

½ recipe Whipped Cream
(see page 126)

*If you layer the pudding as pictured, you will have leftover coconut cream pudding. To use all of both puddings, make slightly thicker layers of coconut cream pudding.

Assembly

1. Prepare coconut cream pudding, and then prepare chocolate pudding. Cool as directed.

2. Toast the coconut: Spread sweetened coconut on a baking sheet and bake in a preheated oven at 350°F for 5–8 minutes. Stir coconut after 3 minutes, and check every minute or so after.

3. Make whipped cream (just before assembly).

4. Alternate layers of chocolate pudding and coconut cream pudding in a dish. Top with fresh whipped cream and toasted coconut.

More Ideas

Not a fan of coconut? Layer the chocolate pudding with vanilla pudding (or vanilla pastry cream, page 115) for an equally beautiful yet simple dessert.

CHOCOLATE-COVERED BANANA DESSERT

Total Time: 3 hours

PREP: 30 minutes

BAKING & COOLING: 2+ hours

ASSEMBLY: 15 minutes

Makes 6–7 servings

Rich chocolate brownie and creamy chocolate pudding reveal a hidden layer of fresh banana.

Dessert Components

Chocolate Pudding
(see page 105)

Fudge Brownies
(see page 87*)

Chocolate Fudge Sauce
(see page 121),
or choose a good-quality
chocolate sauce

½ recipe Whipped Cream
(see page 126),
or use store-bought
whipped cream

2 bananas, sliced

You will have brownie left over.

Assembly

1. Prepare chocolate pudding and allow to chill (at least 2 hours).

2. Bake brownies and allow to cool.

3. If desired, make chocolate fudge sauce, or plan to use store-bought chocolate sauce.

4. When both the pudding and brownies are cool, make whipped cream (or use store-bought whipped cream).

5. Cut brownies into small cubes

6. Begin assembly by adding a layer of brownie to the bottom of each dish. Top with a layer of pudding. Add a layer of sliced banana. Repeat the layers: brownie, pudding, banana. Finish with whipped cream, a drizzle of chocolate sauce, and one slice of banana (just before serving).

More Ideas

Prepare ahead by making the pudding and brownies up to two days in advance, and then assembly will be quick and easy. Or save time by using store-bought brownies and/or prepared pudding.

CHOCOLATE & NUTELLA CREAM DESSERT

Makes 4 servings

Total Time: 3 hours

PREP: 30 minutes

BAKING & COOLING: 2+ hours

ASSEMBLY: 15 minutes

Smooth and creamy chocolate pudding is dressed up with a delicious Nutella cream.

Dessert Components

Chocolate Pudding
(see page 105)

Whipped Cream
(see page 126),
with adjustments

2 Tbsp. Nutella

chocolate pearls, shaved
chocolate, or chopped
hazelnuts, for garnish

Assembly

1. Prepare chocolate pudding and allow to cool (at least 2 hours).

2. When the pudding has cooled, prepare Nutella cream as follows:

3. Make whipped cream, following the general directions on page 126, but use only ¾ cup heavy cream and 3 tablespoons powdered sugar.

4. When the cream is almost fully whipped, slow the mixer to the slowest speed and add ¼ cup cooled chocolate pudding, 1 tablespoon at a time. Then add Nutella, 1 tablespoon at a time. Blend slowly, just until the pudding and Nutella are fully incorporated and the cream is thick and fluffy.

5. Begin dessert assembly by adding a layer of chocolate pudding to each dish. (For the nicest layers, use a piping bag or ziplock bag with a small corner cut off to fill dishes.)

6. Add a layer of Nutella cream. Repeat with another layer of pudding and then more Nutella cream.

7. Garnish with chocolate pearls, shaved chocolate, or chopped hazelnuts.

More Ideas •

The pudding can be made up to 2 days in advance to save time at assembly. Add a layer of chocolate cookie crumble (page 83) or brownie (page 87).

CHOCOLATE MINT CRUNCH

Makes 5-7 servings

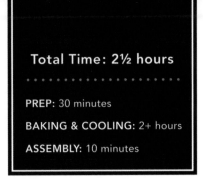

Total Time: 2½ hours

PREP: 30 minutes

BAKING & COOLING: 2+ hours

ASSEMBLY: 10 minutes

Chocolate and mint are the perfect balance of indulgent and refreshing in this dessert that combines creamy and crunchy elements to create a satisfying treat.

Dessert Components

Chocolate Pudding
(see page 105)

Chocolate Cookie Crumble
(see page 83)

Whipped Cream
(see page 126),
with adjustments

chocolate mint candies
(such as Andes mints),
chopped

Assembly

1. Prepare chocolate pudding and allow to cool (at least 2 hours).

2. Prepare chocolate cookie crumble, bake, and cool.

3. Make the whipped cream, adding ½ teaspoon peppermint extract after the cream begins to thicken. At the same time, add 1 drop of green food coloring (if desired). Continue to beat until fully whipped and stiff.

4. Begin assembly by adding 1–2 tablespoons of crumble to the bottom of each dish. Add a few pieces of chopped chocolate mint candy as well.

5. Add a layer of pudding and then the mint whipped cream.

6. Repeat layers: crumble, mints, pudding, cream.

7. Garnish with a few additional pieces of mint candy and cookie crumble.

8. Enjoy immediately, or refrigerate up to 2 hours.

More Ideas

The chocolate pudding can be made up to two days in advance, and the cookie crumble can be made at least a week in advance. With these two elements prepared, the dessert can come together quickly. Replace the chocolate cookie crumble with brownies (page 87), cut into small pieces, for an extra rich treat.

CHOCOLATE OBSESSION

Makes 6 servings

Total Time: 3 hours

PREP: 30 minutes

BAKING & COOLING: 2+ hours

ASSEMBLY: 15 minutes

Layer upon layer of chocolaty goodness will satisfy even the most devoted chocolate fan.

Dessert Components

Chocolate Pudding
(see page 105)

Fudge Brownies
(see page 87*)

Whipped Cream
(see page 126)

You will have brownie left over.

Assembly

1. Prepare chocolate pudding and allow to cool (at least 2 hours).

2. Bake brownies and allow to cool (at least 1 hour).

3. When the pudding and brownies have fully cooled, prepare whipped cream.

4. Once the whipped cream is prepared, gently fold ⅓ cup chocolate pudding (a little at a time) into the whipped cream.

5. Begin assembly by adding a layer of brownie (cut into small cubes) into the bottom of each dish.

6. Add a layer of pudding and then a layer of chocolate whipped cream.

7. Repeat layers: brownie, pudding, chocolate whipped cream.

8. Garnish just before serving with a few small brownie pieces and enjoy immediately. (If you want to prepare this ahead of time, do not add the final brownie garnish, and you can keep the desserts, covered, in the refrigerator up to 4 hours.)

More Ideas •

Replace the brownie layer with chocolate cookie crumble (page 83). For a chocolate, caramel, and cream dessert, keep the whipped cream as is (without chocolate pudding) and add a drizzle of caramel on top of each whipped cream layer.

CHOCOLATE PEANUT BUTTER TRIFLE

Total Time: 3 hours

PREP: 45 minutes

COOLING: 2 hours

ASSEMBLY: 15 minutes

Makes 8-10 servings

This rich and indulgent dessert is sure to be a hit with anyone who loves chocolate and peanut butter.

Dessert Components

Chocolate Pudding
(see page 105)

Fudge Brownies
(see page 87*)

Peanut Butter Mousse
(see page 106)

Whipped Cream
(see page 126)

about ¾ cup chopped mini peanut butter cups

*You will have brownie left over.

Assembly

1. Prepare chocolate pudding and refrigerate (at least 2 hours).

2. Prepare brownies, bake, and cool.

3. Prepare peanut butter mousse.

4. Make whipped cream (just before assembly) and store in the refrigerator.

5. Chop brownies into bite-size cubes. Add a layer of brownie bites and a few chopped peanut butter cups to the bottom of each dessert dish.

6. Add a layer of peanut butter mousse and then a layer of chocolate pudding and a layer of whipped cream.

7. Repeat layers as desired, depending on the size of your dish. Top desserts with a bit of whipped cream and some additional brownie bites and peanut butter cup pieces.

8. Chill desserts at least 15 minutes before serving. The desserts can be stored in the refrigerator up to 4 hours.

More Ideas

If you are short on time, feel free to use a boxed mix to prepare brownies, or use brownies from your store bakery. If desired, you could swap out the homemade chocolate pudding with a pudding mix or prepared pudding. Additionally, you could use nondairy whipped topping (such as Cool Whip) in place of the whipped cream.

CHOCOLATE RASPBERRY CHEESECAKE

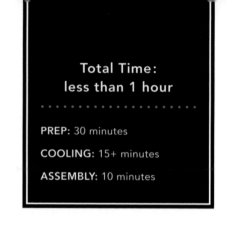

Total Time:
less than 1 hour

. . . .

PREP: 30 minutes

COOLING: 15+ minutes

ASSEMBLY: 10 minutes

Makes 5-6 servings

This rich, elegant dessert is perfect for special occasions but is surprisingly easy to make.

Dessert Components

> **Chocolate Cookie Crumble**
> (see page 83)
>
> **Creamy Whipped Cheesecake**
> (see page 101)
>
> **about 2 cups fresh raspberries**
>
> **Chocolate Ganache**
> (see page 128)

Assembly

1. Prepare chocolate cookie crumble, bake, and cool.

2. Prepare the creamy whipped cheesecake and place in the refrigerator.

3. Rinse and dry fresh raspberries. If the berries are large, slice most of them in half, reserving a few whole to use as garnish.

4. Make chocolate ganache and put in the refrigerator.

5. Begin assembly by adding a layer of crumble to the bottom of each dish (about 2 tablespoons, depending on the size of dish). Press down the crumbs with a small glass (such as a shot glass or a glass spice bottle).

6. Add a layer of raspberry halves and then add a layer of the cheesecake. Place desserts in the refrigerator.

7. When the ganache has slightly thickened but is still pourable, pour a thin layer on top of each dessert dish. Place 1 raspberry on top and move desserts back to the refrigerator. Allow to cool until the chocolate has set (15–30 minutes).

8. The desserts may be kept in the refrigerator up to 4 hours before serving.

COOKIES & CREAM CHEESECAKE

Makes 4–6 servings

Total Time:
less than 1 hour

. . . .

FROM START TO FINISH

The classic flavors of this dessert make it popular with both kids and adults.

Dessert Components

> **Chocolate Cookie Crumble**
> (see page 83)
>
> **Creamy Whipped Cheesecake**
> (see page 101)
>
> **Whipped Cream, as garnish**
> (see page 126), optional

Assembly

1. Prepare and bake chocolate cookie crumble and cool.

2. Prepare creamy whipped cheesecake. When the cheesecake mixture is complete, add in ⅓ cup chocolate cookie crumble and blend until well combined.

3. If desired, prepare whipped cream.

4. Assemble the desserts by adding about 2 tablespoons chocolate cookie crumble to the bottom of each dish. Top crumbs with a layer of the cheesecake. (Assembly may be easiest if you fill a large ziplock bag with the cheesecake, cut off one corner of the bag, and squeeze out the cheesecake into the dishes.)

5. Add another layer of chocolate cookie crumble and then another layer of cheesecake.

6. If desired, top with a dollop of whipped cream and a piece of cookie.

7. Store the desserts in the refrigerator until ready to serve. Best when chilled about 15 minutes. Enjoy within 4 hours of assembly for best texture.

CREAMY NO-BAKE CHEESECAKE WITH BLUEBERRY SAUCE

Total Time: 3½ hours

PREP: 30 minutes

CHILLING: 3 hours

ASSEMBLY: 5 minutes

Makes 6–8 servings

This creamy and delicious cheesecake is dressed with gorgeous homemade blueberry sauce.

Dessert Components

homemade blueberry sauce
(see page 122)

Graham Cracker Crumble
(see page 84)

Creamy No-Bake Cheesecake
(see page 108)

Assembly

1. Prepare blueberry sauce and cool in the refrigerator.

2. Prepare graham cracker crumble, bake, and cool.

3. Prepare creamy no-bake cheesecake.

4. Add a layer of graham cracker crumble to the bottom of each dish (2–3 tablespoons, depending on the size of dish). Pour or spoon a layer of cheesecake on top of the crumble.

5. Chill cheesecake about 2 hours.

6. Add blueberry sauce just before serving or anytime after the cheesecake has fully chilled.

7. This is a great make-ahead dessert and can be made up to 1 day in advance and stored in the refrigerator. When making ahead, keep topping separate until shortly before serving.

More Ideas

This cheesecake base is very versatile and is delicious topped with most any fruit topping. To save time, feel free to use fruit pie filling (such as blueberry or cherry) in place of the homemade fruit sauce. As another alternative, you can make a quick fresh fruit topping by mixing fresh fruit (such as blueberries, raspberries, blackberries, chopped strawberries, or cherries) with about 1 tablespoon of sugar. Stir together and place fruit in the refrigerator until ready to use (chill at least 15 minutes before use).

FRESH FRUIT CHEESECAKE MOUSSE

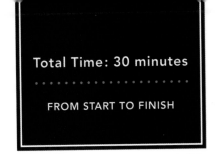

Total Time: 30 minutes

· · · · · · · · · · · · · · · · · · · ·

FROM START TO FINISH

Makes 4 servings

This easy dessert looks extra nice in tall glasses so you can show off the beautiful layers of fresh fruit.

Dessert Components

Cheesecake Mousse
(see page 101)

fresh fruit of choice
(blueberries, mango, kiwifruit, and strawberries are shown)

Assembly

1. Prepare cheesecake mousse. Cool in the refrigerator while you prepare fruit.

2. Peel and chop fresh fruit as needed.

3. Start with the fruit of your choice in the bottom of each glass. Add a layer of cheesecake mousse and then repeat with another layer of fruit and another layer of cheesecake mousse. Assembly may be easiest if you fill a large ziplock bag with the cheesecake, cut off one corner of the bag, and squeeze the cheesecake into the dishes.

4. Continue layering cheesecake and fruit depending on the size of your glass and the variety of fruit.

More Ideas ·

Feel free to mix and match fruits of your choice. Berries, cherries, peaches, mango, or pineapple would all be good choices. Make a tropical cheesecake trifle using mango, pineapple, and kiwifruit and top with toasted coconut.

FRIED ICE CREAM CHEESECAKE

Makes 5-6 servings

Total Time: 30 minutes

· · · · · · · · · · · · · · · · · ·

FROM START TO FINISH

Inspired by fried ice cream, often served at Mexican restaurants, creamy cheesecake is layered with cinnamon sugar cereal for an unexpected twist.

Dessert Components

2 cups cinnamon cereal
(such as Cinnamon Toast Crunch)

2 Tbsp. butter

Creamy Whipped Cheesecake
(see page 101),
with adjustments

½ recipe Whipped Cream
(see page 126)

6 maraschino cherries

Assembly

1. Crush cinnamon cereal in a large ziplock bag and then place crushed cereal in a bowl. Melt 2 tablespoons butter and pour over cereal. Stir well. Spread cereal onto a baking sheet and bake at 350°F for 6–8 minutes. Allow to cool.

2. Prepare creamy whipped cheesecake—omit lemon zest and add ½ teaspoon cinnamon.

3. Assemble dessert by adding 1–2 tablespoons crushed cereal to the bottom of your dessert dishes. Add a layer of cheesecake (this will be easiest if you use a piping bag fitted with a large round tip, or add cheesecake to a large ziplock bag and snip off one corner). Repeat with another layer of cereal and then more cheesecake. Top with whipped cream and a cherry.

4. Enjoy immediately or keep in the refrigerator (up to 1 hour).

More Ideas ·

If desired, you can skip the step of baking the cereal and use the crushed cereal as is (with no butter).

KEY LIME COCONUT CHEESECAKE

Makes 6-8 servings

Total Time: 3½ hours

PREP: 30 minutes

CHILLING: 3+ hours

ASSEMBLY: 15 minutes

This creamy, sweet, and tart cheesecake is a perfect summer dessert.

Dessert Components

> **Coconut Graham Cracker Crumble**
> (see page 84)
>
> **Key Lime Cheesecake**
> (see page 113)
>
> **about ¾ cup coconut**
>
> **½ recipe Whipped Cream**
> (see page 126),
> garnish

Assembly

1. Prepare coconut graham cracker crumble, bake, and cool.

2. Prepare key lime cheesecake.

3. Add about 2 tablespoons crumble into the bottom of each dish (more or less depending on the size of dish).

4. Pour or scoop the cheesecake mixture on top of the crumble. Cover and chill at least 3 hours, or overnight.

5. To toast coconut, lay desired amount on a baking sheet and bake in a preheated oven at 350°F for 5–8 minutes. Stir coconut after 3 minutes and check on it every minute or so after.

6. Prepare whipped cream (or use canned whipped cream).

7. Garnish dishes with whipped cream and toasted coconut just before serving.

LEMON BLUEBERRY TRIFLE

Makes 6-8 servings

Total Time: 2 hours

PREP: 45 minutes

BAKING & COOLING: 1 hour

ASSEMBLY: 15 minutes

Light and fluffy sponge cake, fresh berries, and whipped lemon cream create a dessert that is perfect for a warm summer day.

Dessert Components

Lemon Curd
(see page 125),
to be added to
whipped lemon cream

Vanilla Sponge Cake
(see page 95)

Whipped Lemon Cream
(see page 128)

1–1½ cups fresh blueberries

lemon zest
(optional)

Assembly

1. Prepare lemon curd and cool (or use store-bought lemon curd).

2. Prepare vanilla sponge cake, bake, and cool.

3. Prepare whipped lemon cream.

4. Assemble dessert by starting with a layer of sponge cake (cut into small cubes). Add several blueberries and then a layer of whipped lemon cream. Repeat layers: cake, blueberries, lemon cream.

5. Garnish with a few berries, a piece of cake, and some lemon zest (optional).

6. Enjoy immediately.

More Ideas •

For a different flavor combination, try raspberries in place of the blueberries. To save time, feel free to replace the vanilla sponge cake with store-bought angel food cake or pound cake. You could also replace the homemade lemon curd with store-bought lemon curd (available near jams and jellies).

LEMONS ON A CLOUD

Total Time: 45 minutes

FROM START TO FINISH

Makes 4–5 servings

Sweet, tart, and light as a cloud, this lemony dessert is perfect after a rich meal.

Dessert Components

> **Lemon Curd**
> (see page 125)
>
> **Graham Cracker Crumble**
> (see page 84)
>
> **Yogurt Cream**
> (see below)
>
> **lemon zest**
> (optional)

Assembly

1. Make lemon curd and cool in the refrigerator.

2. Prepare graham cracker crumble, bake, and cool.

3. Prepare yogurt cream.

4. Layer components in dessert dishes: start with a layer of graham cracker crumble, then yogurt cream, and then a thin layer of lemon curd. Repeat layers. Garnish with a bit of fresh lemon zest, if desired. Assembled desserts can be stored in the refrigerator up to 2 hours before serving.

YOGURT CREAM

Components

> ²/₃ cup heavy cream
>
> ½ cup powdered sugar
>
> ½ tsp. vanilla
>
> ¾ cup (6-oz.) plain Greek yogurt
> (any fat content)

Directions

In the bowl of an electric mixer, beat the heavy cream until it begins to thicken. While mixing, slowly add powdered sugar and then vanilla. Continue to beat until mixture is thickened and holds a stiff peak. Gently fold yogurt into the whipped cream (using a spatula). Use immediately, or chill until ready to assemble dessert.

More Ideas

For a sweeter, slightly richer dessert, replace the yogurt cream with cheesecake mousse (page 101).

MANGO LIME COCONUT CHEESECAKE

Makes 6–8 servings

Total Time: 3½ hours

PREP: 30 minutes

CHILLING: 3+ hours

ASSEMBLY: 15 minutes

The fresh and tropical flavors of this dessert were inspired by a delicious cheesecake a friend and I once shared at a restaurant. The balance of sweet and tart, rich and fruity, creates a memorable dessert.

Dessert Components

Coconut Graham
Cracker Crumble
(see page 84)

about ¾ cup
sweetened coconut

Key Lime Cheesecake
(see page 113)

Mango Puree
(see page 107)

½ recipe Whipped Cream
(see page 126),
or use canned whipped cream

lime zest
(optional)

Assembly

1. Prepare coconut graham cracker crumble, bake, and cool.

2. While the oven is still on, toast the coconut: spread sweetened coconut on a baking sheet and bake in a preheated oven at 350°F for 5–8 minutes. Stir coconut after 3 minutes and check every minute or so after.

3. Prepare key lime cheesecake. Set the cheesecake in the refrigerator and allow to chill while you finish preparations. (The cheesecake portion should chill at least 3 hours before serving. You can prepare the crust and the cheesecake, and keep it in the fridge up to 1 day, and then prepare the mango puree and whipped cream shortly before serving. Or, prepare the full dessert [excluding garnish], chill about 3 hours, and then serve.)

4. Make mango puree.

5. Make whipped cream, or plan to use canned whipped cream.

6. Begin assembly by adding a layer of coconut graham cracker crumble to the bottom of each dish (about 2 tablespoons, depending on the size of your dish).

7. Add a portion of cheesecake. Top with a thin layer of mango puree. Garnish with whipped cream, toasted coconut, and a bit of lime zest (if desired).

NUTELLA & BANANA TRIFLE

Makes 4 servings

Total Time: 1½ hours

PREP: 20 minutes

BAKING & COOLING: 1+ hours

ASSEMBLY: 10 minutes

The classic flavors of a Nutella and banana crepe were the inspiration for this trifle.

Dessert Components

Vanilla Sponge Cake
(see page 95*)

Nutella Cream
(see below)

½ recipe Whipped Cream
(see page 126)

2 bananas

*You will have cake left over.

NUTELLA CREAM

Components

4 oz. cream cheese
(½ block)

⅓ cup Nutella
(hazelnut spread)

½ cup heavy cream

½ tsp. vanilla extract

⅓ cup powdered sugar

Assembly

1. Bake vanilla sponge cake, and allow to cool.

2. Prepare Nutella cream and put in the refrigerator until ready to assemble dessert.

3. Prepare whipped cream (or you can use canned whipped cream).

4. Cut sponge cake into small cubes and then slice bananas.

5. Assemble desserts by adding a layer of sponge cake and then a layer of nutella cream. Add a layer of banana slices. Repeat layers: cake, Nutella cream, bananas. Garnish with whipped cream.

6. Enjoy dessert immediately.

Directions

In the bowl of an electric mixer, blend cream cheese until smooth (using the whip attachment). Add Nutella and blend until fully incorporated. Continue mixing and slowly pour in heavy cream. Beat until the cream is fully incorporated and the mixture has thickened and increased in volume. Add vanilla and slowly add powdered sugar (while mixing). Mix until all of the ingredients are well blended and the mixture is light and fluffy. Use at once, or place in the refrigerator (up to 2 hours).

More Ideas

Replace the vanilla sponge cake with brownie (page 87) for an extra-rich treat.

ORANGE VANILLA PANNA COTTA

Makes 6–8 servings

Total Time: 2 hours

PREP: 45 minutes

CHILLING: 1 hour

ASSEMBLY: 15 minutes

This delicious and eye-catching dessert can be made in advance and is an especially refreshing treat during warm weather.

Dessert Components

Vanilla Panna Cotta
(see page 111)

¾ cup orange marmalade

2 Tbsp. orange juice
(or water)

1 drop orange food coloring
(optional)

More Ideas ......

You can save time by having just one layer of panna cotta, with a layer of orange sauce on the top and bottom. Almost any fruit sauce can be used as a topping or layered with this panna cotta. Try the home-made blueberry sauce (page 122) or your favorite preserves.

Assembly

1. Prepare vanilla panna cotta and temporarily place entire pot of panna cotta in the refrigerator.

2. Make orange sauce by heating orange marmalade with orange juice (or water) together in a small saucepan (or in the microwave). Stir well to combine and then strain mixture through a fine strainer to remove the large pieces of orange peel. Allow to cool. If desired, you may want to add a small drop of orange food coloring to enhance the color.

3. Begin assembly by adding a small amount of orange sauce to the bottom of each dessert dish. Place dishes in the freezer 5–10 minutes, just until slightly firm.

4. Slowly pour a layer of the panna cotta on top of the orange sauce. Again move to the freezer, and freeze 30–45 minutes, until set on the top.

5. Repeat layers, slowly adding a layer of orange sauce, freezing just until set, and then adding a second layer of panna cotta. Freeze until just set and then add a finishing layer of orange sauce. Keep in the refrigerator until ready to serve.

6. During this process, you can keep the orange sauce at room temperature and keep the panna cotta (in the pan) in the refrigerator.

PEACH RASPBERRY ALMOND TRIFLE

Makes 6–7 servings

Total Time: 1½ hours

PREP: 30 minutes

BAKING & COOLING: 1 hour

ASSEMBLY: 15 minutes

This fresh and flavorful trifle would be a beautiful addition to a brunch menu, or it is perfect as a summer dessert.

Dessert Components

Vanilla Sponge Cake
(see page 95)

Creamy Whipped Cheesecake
(see page 101),
with adjustments

1–2 large fresh peaches

2 cups fresh raspberries

about ¾ cup sliced almonds

Assembly

1. Prepare, bake, and cool vanilla sponge cake.

2. While the oven is still on, toast the almonds: spread sliced almonds onto a baking sheet and bake in a preheated oven at 350°F for 5–8 minutes, or until light golden brown.

3. While the cake cools, prepare creamy whipped cheesecake, but increase heavy cream to 1 cup, add 1 teaspoon almond extract, and omit lemon zest. Place whipped cheesecake mixture in the refrigerator.

4. Shortly before serving, peel and dice peaches.

5. Begin assembly by adding a layer of sponge cake (cut into small cubes). Add a layer of peaches and raspberries and a few toasted almonds. Top with a layer of whipped cheesecake. Repeat layers: cake, fruit, cheesecake.

6. Garnish with a few sliced almonds and a raspberry.

More Ideas • • • • • • • • • • • • • • • •

Save time by replacing the vanilla sponge cake with a store-bought angel food cake or pound cake.

PEACHES & CREAM

Makes 6 servings

Total Time: 30 minutes

FROM START TO FINISH

This simple yet beautiful dessert is the perfect way to enjoy fresh summer peaches.

Dessert Components

> 2 large fresh peaches or nectarines
>
> 1 Tbsp. sugar
>
> Cheesecake Mousse
> (see page 101)

Assembly

1. Peel and chop peaches into bite-size pieces (about ½-inch cubes). If using nectarines (as shown), there is no need to peel them.

2. Place chopped fruit in a bowl and sprinkle with 1 tablespoon of sugar. Stir together, cover, and place the bowl in the refrigerator (about 15 minutes).

3. Prepare cheesecake mousse.

4. Assemble by adding a portion of cheesecake mousse to each dish and topping with a large spoonful of peaches.

5. Serve immediately or keep in the refrigerator up to 1 hour. (The cheesecake mousse can be prepared up to 1 day in advance and kept in the refrigerator, but it's best to add the fruit shortly before serving.)

More Ideas •

Use a taller dish to create more layers.

PEANUT BUTTER MOUSSE WITH CHOCOLATE COOKIE CRUMBLE

Makes 6-7 servings

Chocolate and peanut butter is a match made in heaven—this simple dessert celebrates these two rich and delicious flavors!

Dessert Components

Chocolate Cookie Crumble
(see page 83)

Peanut Butter Mousse
(see page 106)

mini peanut butter cups,
garnish

Assembly

1. Prepare chocolate cookie crumble, bake, and cool.

2. Prepare peanut butter mousse.

3. Add 1–2 tablespoons crumble to the bottom of your dishes (depending on size of dish). Spoon or pipe a layer of the peanut butter mousse. Repeat layers of crumble and mousse, as desired. Top with a small amount of crumble and a mini peanut butter cup.

4. Refrigerate desserts at least 15 minutes. The dessert can be made ahead up to 4 hours. Add final crumble topping just before serving (if storing more than 15 minutes).

PIÑA COLADA CHEESECAKE MOUSSE

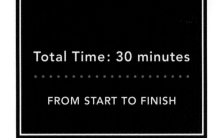

Makes 4–6 servings

This cool and refreshing treat will make you feel like you're on a tropical vacation.

Dessert Components

> **Coconut Graham Cracker Crumble**
> (see page 84)
>
> **½ cup sweetened coconut**
>
> **Pineapple Cheesecake Mousse**
> (see page 98)
>
> **½ recipe Whipped Cream**
> (see page 126),
> garnish
>
> **maraschino cherries**
> (optional)
>
> **fresh pineapple slices**
> (optional)

Assembly

1. Prepare coconut graham cracker crumble and allow to cool.

2. Toast coconut by spreading coconut onto rimmed baking sheet and baking in an oven at 350°F for 5–8 minutes. Stir coconut after 3 minutes and check on it every minute or so after.

3. Prepare pineapple cheesecake mousse.

4. Add a layer of coconut graham cracker crumble to the bottom of each dish (about 2 tablespoons, depending on the size of your dish). Top with a portion of pineapple cheesecake mousse. Refrigerate dessert for 15 minutes.

5. Prepare whipped cream (or use canned whipped cream).

6. Garnish with whipped cream and toasted coconut. Add a maraschino cherry and/or a slice of fresh pineapple if desired.

PUMPKIN CARAMEL BANANA TRIFLE

Makes 8–9 servings

Classic, comforting flavors of caramel, pumpkin, and banana create beautiful layers in this delicious dessert.

Total Time: 2½ hours

PREP: 30 minutes

BAKING: 45 minutes

COOLING: 1+ hours

ASSEMBLY: 15 minutes

Dessert Components

Pumpkin Spice Cake
(see page 91*)

Caramel Sauce
(see page 118)

Whipped Cream
(see page 126)

3–4 bananas

You will have cake left over.

Assembly

1. Prepare pumpkin spice cake, bake, and cool.
2. Make caramel sauce and allow to cool. (You could use a good-quality store-bought caramel sauce in place of the homemade.)
3. Make whipped cream.
4. Just before assembly, slice bananas.
5. Add a layer of pumpkin cake (cut into small cubes) in the bottom of each dessert dish. Top with a few slices of banana and drizzle with caramel sauce.
6. Add a layer of whipped cream.
7. Repeat layers: cake, bananas, caramel, whipped cream.
8. Garnish with a slice of banana, a few small pieces of cake, and a drizzle of caramel.
9. Enjoy immediately.

More Ideas

The caramel sauce can be made at least 1 week in advance, the cake can be made up to 3 days in advance, and the whipped cream can be made several hours in advance (and stored in the refrigerator). If you have these ingredients prepared ahead of time, assembly will be quick. Also, try adding an additional element of texture by including some toasted nuts, such as pecans.

PUMPKIN MOUSSE PARFAIT

Makes 8–10 servings

Total Time: 45 minutes

PREP: 20 minutes

CHILLING: 15 minutes

ASSEMBLY: 10 minutes

Creamy spiced pumpkin mousse, a nutty crumble, and whipped cream come together in this delicious dessert, perfect for fall entertaining.

Dessert Components

Cinnamon Nut Crumble
(see page 84)

Pumpkin Mousse
(see page 116)

Whipped Cream
(see page 126)

Assembly

1. Prepare crumble, bake, and cool.

2. Make pumpkin mousse.

3. Make whipped cream.

4. Add about 2 tablespoons crumble to the bottom of each dish. Add a layer of pumpkin mousse and then a layer of whipped cream. Repeat layers: crumble, pumpkin mousse, whipped cream. Garnish with an extra bit of crumble.

5. Chill the finished desserts for 15 minutes before serving. Desserts may be kept in the refrigerator up to 4 hours before serving.

More Ideas •

Don't care for nuts? Feel free to replace the cinnamon nut crumble with graham cracker crumble (page 84).

PUMPKIN SPICE CAKE TRIFLE

Makes 6-7 servings

Flavorful pumpkin cake, creamy whipped filling, and crunchy pecans create a delicious trifle full of fall flavors.

Total Time: 2½ hours

PREP: 30 minutes

BAKING & COOLING: 2 hours

ASSEMBLY: 15 minutes

Dessert Components

Pumpkin Spice Cake
(see page 91*)

Sugared Nuts
(see page 92*)

Creamy Whipped Cheesecake
(see page 101),
with adjustments

*You will have cake and nuts left over.

Assembly

1. Make pumpkin spice cake and allow to cool (can be made up to 2 days in advance).

2. Make sugared nuts and allow to cool (can be made up to 1 week in advance).

3. When the cake is cool, prepare creamy whipped cheesecake, but increase heavy cream to 1 cup.

4. Begin assembly by adding a layer of pumpkin cake (cut into small cubes) in the bottom of each dish.

5. Add a few sugared nuts and then a layer of creamy whipped cheesecake.

6. Repeat the layers: cake, nuts, cream. Garnish with a few nuts and 1–2 cubes of cake.

7. Enjoy immediately. (If you need to prepare these ahead of time, cover and keep refrigerated up to 2 hours, but do not add the final garnish of cake until just before serving.)

RASPBERRY BLACKBERRY CHEESECAKE MOUSSE

Total Time: 30 minutes

PREP & ASSEMBLY: 15 minutes
CHILLING: 15 minutes

Makes 6 servings

This light and fluffy berry dessert is extra pretty due to the two-tone layers.

Dessert Components

Raspberry & Blackberry Cheesecake Mousses
(see page 112)

Fresh raspberries or blackberries,
garnish

Assembly

1. Prepare raspberry and blackberry cheesecake mousses. Scoop or pipe mixtures in alternating layers into dessert dishes. Depending on your dishes, you may do 2, 3, or 4 layers. If you do 3 layers (as shown), then some dishes will need to have 2 layers of raspberry and 1 layer of blackberry, and other dishes will have 2 layers of blackberry and 1 layer of raspberry.

2. Chill for 15 minutes or up to 2 hours.

3. Garnish with fresh raspberries or blackberries before serving.

Note: Depending on how deeply colored your blackberries are, you may want to add 1 drop of purple food coloring so there is a clear visual difference between the raspberry and blackberry layers.

STRAWBERRIES ON A CHOCOLATE CLOUD

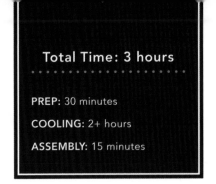

Total Time: 3 hours

PREP: 30 minutes

COOLING: 2+ hours

ASSEMBLY: 15 minutes

Makes 7–8 servings

The combination of chocolate and strawberries is always a hit! This dessert starts with delicious chocolate mousse and then dresses it up with sweet strawberries and whipped cream.

Dessert Components

Chocolate Mousse
(see page 102)

**2 baskets/pints
fresh strawberries**

1 Tbsp. sugar

½ recipe Whipped Cream
(see page 126),
or use canned whipped cream

semisweet chocolate,
to dip strawberries for
garnish (optional)

Assembly

1. Prepare chocolate mousse. (Note: The mousse requires about 2 hours of chilling.)

2. When the chocolate mousse is complete, wash and chop the strawberries. Place chopped strawberries in a bowl and sprinkle sugar over berries. Stir, and then cover bowl and place in the fridge (10–15 minutes).

3. Make whipped cream (or plan to use canned whipped cream).

4. Fill your dessert dishes about ⅔ full with chocolate mousse. Add a layer of strawberries and then top with whipped cream.

5. Garnish with a whole strawberry or chocolate-dipped strawberry, if desired.

6. Enjoy immediately, or keep in the refrigerator up to 2 hours.

STRAWBERRY CHEESECAKE MOUSSE

Total Time: 30 minutes

· ·

PREP: 15 minutes

CHILLING: 15 minutes

Makes 6 servings

This light and fresh treat is perfect for a spring or summer dessert.

Dessert Components

⅔ cup heavy cream

¾ cup powdered sugar,
divided

1 (8-oz.) block cream cheese

1 tsp. vanilla

½ cup strawberry puree,
made from about 1 cup fresh
or frozen strawberries

fresh strawberries,
chopped for garnish

Assembly

1. In the bowl of an electric mixer, beat the heavy cream until it begins to thicken. While mixing, slowly add ¼ cup of the powdered sugar. Continue to beat until mixture is thickened and holds a stiff peak. Do not overbeat or it will become overly thick and clumpy. Scoop mixture into a bowl and put in the refrigerator.

2. In the empty mixer (no need to wash), add cream cheese and beat until smooth. Continue mixing and add remaining powdered sugar and vanilla. Add strawberry puree, a little at a time, while slowly mixing. Stop mixing and gently fold in (with a spatula) the cold whipped cream. Fold together until just combined.

3. Scoop the cheesecake mixture into dessert dishes. Top with chopped strawberries.

More Ideas ·

The options with this dessert are endless! Feel free to add a crust layer, such as graham cracker crumble (page 84), or try this recipe with cherries or peaches. Raspberries and blackberries are shown on page 72.

SUMMER BERRY TRIFLE

Makes 8-10 servings

Total Time: 3 hours

PREP: 30 minutes

BAKING & COOLING: 2+ hours

ASSEMBLY: 15 minutes

This fresh and colorful trifle is perfect for a summer picnic or barbecue.

Dessert Components

Vanilla Pastry Cream
(see page 115)

Vanilla Sponge Cake
(see page 95)

3 cups mixed fresh berries
(strawberries, raspberries, blackberries, and blueberries shown)

½ recipe Whipped Cream
(see page 126), garnish

Assembly

1. Prepare vanilla pastry cream and place in the refrigerator to cool (about 3 hours).

2. Prepare vanilla sponge cake, bake, and cool.

3. When the pastry cream and cake have both cooled, wash and cut fruit.

4. Make whipped cream (or use canned whipped cream).

5. Assemble the dessert by adding a layer of cake (cut into bite-size cubes) and then a layer of fresh fruit. Top the fruit with a layer of pastry cream. Repeat layers: cake, fruit, pastry cream.

6. Garnish with whipped cream and some additional fruit.

7. Enjoy immediately, or within 2 hours of assembly. (The sponge cake and the pastry cream can be made 1–2 days in advance.)

More Ideas

Mix and match fresh fruit of your choice (cherries, peaches, berries, and so on). You can also save time by using store-bought angel food cake or pound cake in place of the homemade sponge cake. Additionally, feel free to replace the homemade vanilla pastry cream with vanilla pudding.

Essential Recipes

This collection of recipes contains the basic components for each of the finished layered desserts. I am sure you will find there are countless more ways to mix and match these recipes, and many of the recipes are quite delicious on their own.

I believe you'll find that in most cases the flavor of these from-scratch desserts surpasses their store-bought counterparts, but feel free to mix and match with the listed "store-bought swaps" as time demands.

Crusts, Cakes & Crumbles

CHOCOLATE COOKIE CRUMBLE

Makes 2 cups

This simple chocolate cookie crust is a delicious base for countless desserts.

Ingredients

> **17 chocolate sandwich cookies** (such as Oreos)
>
> **3 Tbsp. butter**

Directions

1. Preheat oven to 350°F.

2. Use a rolling pin to crush cookies (cookie and cream) in a large ziplock bag. Or, if desired, chop the cookies in a food processor. Using a food processor will produce finer crumbs. It's up to you how small you want the crumbs or if you want to leave a few pieces a bit larger.

3. Place cookie crumbs in a large bowl.

4. Melt butter in a small bowl in the microwave.

5. Pour melted butter over cookie crumbs and stir until crumbs are evenly moistened.

6. Spread crumbs onto a rimmed baking sheet and bake for 10 minutes.

7. Store crumble in a sealed container for up to 1 week.

GRAHAM CRACKER CRUMBLE

Makes 2 cups

This versatile crust is a perfect way to add some texture to a variety of layered desserts. Try one of the variations listed below to add another dimension of flavor.

Ingredients

1 sleeve (9 whole crackers) **graham crackers,** or about 1¾ cups graham cracker crumbs

1 Tbsp. sugar

6 Tbsp. butter

Directions

1. Preheat oven to 350°F.
2. Crush graham crackers in a large ziplock bag and then pour into a large bowl. Add sugar and stir to combine.
3. In a small bowl, melt butter in the microwave.
4. Pour melted butter over bowl of crumbs and stir until the crumbs are evenly moistened.
5. Spread crumbs onto a rimmed baking sheet and bake 8–10 minutes.
6. Allow to cool before use.
7. Crumble can be stored in a sealed container up to 1 week.

VARIATIONS ••••••••••••••••••••••••••••••••••••••

Cinnamon Nut Crumble

Follow the recipe above, but add 1 cup chopped nuts (pecans shown) and ½ teaspoon ground cinnamon to mixture before baking.

Coconut Graham Cracker Crumble

Follow the recipe above, but add 1½ cups sweetened shredded coconut to the mixture before baking.

FUDGE BROWNIES

Makes 1 (9×9) pan

Sometimes there is nothing better than a rich and fudgy brownie! Once you make a batch of these delicious brownies, you'll find lots of excuses to make them again and again.

Ingredients

10 Tbsp. butter
(1 stick plus 2 tablespoons)

1½ cups sugar

3 eggs

¾ cup unsweetened
cocoa powder

¾ tsp. baking powder

¾ tsp. salt

2 tsp. vanilla extract

1 cup flour

1 cup semisweet
chocolate chips

Store-Bought Swap

Feel free to use baked brownies from the grocery store, or a brownie box mix, as a replacement in any recipe that calls for brownies.

Directions

1. Preheat oven to 350°F. Line the bottom and 2 sides of a 9×9 pan with a sheet of parchment paper, leaving a bit of an overhang of paper. Butter the 2 unlined sides.

2. In a medium bowl, add butter and sugar. Heat the butter and sugar in the microwave (or the top of a double boiler) until butter is melted and sugar is beginning to dissolve. Stir to combine and then set aside to cool.

3. In a large bowl, whisk eggs. Add cocoa powder, baking powder, salt, and vanilla. Stir to fully combine.

4. Add cooled (or just slightly warm) butter/sugar mixture to egg/cocoa mixture, stirring until smooth.

5. Add the flour and chocolate chips to batter and stir until fully incorporated.

6. Spread batter into prepared pan and smooth as needed.

7. Bake brownies 22–25 minutes. Test brownies for doneness by inserting a toothpick in the center of the pan and removing. The toothpick should reveal a few moist crumbs but no wet batter.

8. Cool completely before cutting. Run a knife along the sides of the pan and then pull up on the parchment paper to remove the brownies from the pan.

9. Store brownies wrapped tightly in plastic wrap, or in a sealed container, up to 3 days. Baked brownies can also be frozen.

OATMEAL NUT CRUMBLE

Makes 3 cups

This sweet and crunchy crumble pairs wonderfully with fruit and is a delicious complement to pumpkin desserts as well.

Ingredients

½ cup butter

1 cup old-fashioned oats

¾ cup chopped nuts
(pecans shown)

½ cup flour

½ cup brown sugar

¼ tsp. salt

½ tsp. cinnamon

⅛ tsp. nutmeg
(freshly grated, if possible)

Directions

1. Preheat oven to 350°F.

2. Melt butter in a small bowl in the microwave and then set aside.

3. In a large bowl, add remaining ingredients.

4. Pour melted butter on top of the oat mixture and stir until well incorporated.

5. Spread mixture onto a rimmed baking sheet and bake for 10–12 minutes.

6. Allow to cool before use.

Store-Bought Swap • • • • • • • • • • • • • • • • • • •

In recipes that call for this crumble, feel free to substitute with a store-bought granola cereal of your choice.

PUMPKIN SPICE CAKE

Makes 1 (9×9) pan

This moist and flavorful spice cake is delicious on its own and is also a great component to layer in fall-inspired trifles.

Ingredients

2½ cups flour

1½ tsp. baking soda

½ tsp. baking powder

½ tsp. salt

1½ tsp. cinnamon

½ tsp. ground ginger

½ tsp. nutmeg

¼ tsp. cloves

½ cup vegetable oil

2 eggs

1½ cups sugar

1 (15-oz.) can pumpkin puree

1 tsp. vanilla extract

Directions

1. Preheat oven to 350°F. Butter a 9×9 baking pan.

2. In a large bowl, whisk flour, baking soda, baking powder, salt, cinnamon, ginger, nutmeg, and cloves.

3. In another large bowl, whisk (by hand) oil, eggs, sugar, pumpkin puree, and vanilla. Whisk until well incorporated.

4. Add dry ingredients to pumpkin mixture and stir just until fully combined.

5. Pour batter into prepared pan and spread to level batter.

6. Bake 40–45 minutes, or until a toothpick inserted in the center comes out with just a few moist crumbs but no wet batter.

7. Allow to cool.

8. Store cake at room temperature, covered, up to 3 days. Or the cake can be frozen. To freeze cake, cool fully and then wrap well. Defrost cake at room temperature (while still wrapped).

More Ideas •

Slice the cake into thin ¾-inch slices, vertically, and serve as you would pumpkin bread. This cake is perfect for a special breakfast or brunch.

SUGARED NUTS

Makes 3½ cups

This addictive treat is delicious by the handful but is also a beautiful garnish or crumb crust alternative. For most any recipe that calls for graham cracker crumble, you could chop up these baked nuts and use in place of the crumble.

Ingredients

1 cup sugar

1 tsp. cinnamon

¼ tsp. nutmeg
(freshly grated, if possible)

1 tsp. salt

1 egg white

1 Tbsp. water

1 tsp. vanilla

3 cups nuts
(pecans shown)

Directions

1. Preheat oven to 300°F.

2. Line a baking sheet with a silicone baking mat, or lightly spray a baking sheet with nonstick spray.

3. In a small bowl, mix sugar, cinnamon, nutmeg, and salt and set aside.

4. In the bowl of your electric mixer, beat egg white and water on medium-high speed until stiff peaks form, about 4–5 minutes.

5. Add vanilla and then add bowl of sugar and spices. Stir to combine.

6. Add nuts to the bowl and stir with a large spoon or spatula until the nuts are fully coated.

7. Spread nuts onto prepared baking sheet.

8. Bake for 45 minutes, stirring every 15 minutes.

9. Allow to cool. Store the nuts in a sealed container, at room temperature, up to 2 weeks.

VANILLA SPONGE CAKE

Makes 1 loaf

This flavorful yet light-as-air cake is similar to angel food cake. This recipe comes together quite quickly and is a delicious addition to many layered desserts. For a super simple dessert, just top a slice of this cake with whipped cream and fresh strawberries (or other fruit).

Ingredients

3 eggs

¼ tsp. cream of tartar

2 Tbsp. water

½ cup sugar

1 tsp. vanilla extract

¼ tsp. salt

½ cup cake flour

Store-Bought Swap

For any recipe that calls for vanilla sponge cake, you could use store-bought angel food cake or pound cake.

Directions

1. Preheat oven to 325°F. Line the bottom of a 9×5 loaf pan with parchment paper (or rub with butter). Do not line or grease the sides of the pan.

2. Separate the eggs, with the whites in one bowl and the yolks in another bowl. Using an electric mixer, whip the egg whites with the cream of tartar and water until the mixture has greatly increased in volume, is thick, and holds a stiff peak. (To test, lift the beater from the bowl and a mountain-like "peak" should remain still.) Move the fluffy egg whites to a separate bowl.

3. In the bowl of your electric mixer (no need to wash the bowl), add the egg yolks and sugar and beat until creamy, light yellow, and thickened. Add vanilla and salt and mix to combine. Add the flour, and mix until just combined.

4. Gently fold the egg whites into the batter (using a spatula)—a little at first and then a large scoop at a time. Fold just until the egg whites and batter are combined. Do not overmix or the egg whites will lose their volume.

5. Pour batter into the prepared pan and bake for 40–42 minutes.

6. Use a toothpick to check that the cake is done—a toothpick gently inserted in the center of the cake should come out clean, or with a few crumbs, but no wet batter.

7. Cool cake completely before removing from pan. Cut slices with a serrated knife and wipe clean between cuts for best results. Once fully cool, the cake can be stored (loosely covered) at room temperature up to 2 days.

Fillings, Puddings & Cheesecakes

PINEAPPLE CHEESECAKE MOUSSE

Pictured on page 65

Makes 3½ cups

Ingredients

⅔ cup heavy cream

¾ cup powdered sugar, divided

1 (8-oz.) block cream cheese

1 tsp. vanilla

½ cup crushed (canned) pineapple, drained

Directions

1. In the bowl of an electric mixer, beat the heavy cream until it begins to thicken. While mixing, slowly add ¼ cup powdered sugar. Continue to beat until mixture is thickened and holds a stiff peak. Do not overbeat or it will become overly thick and clumpy. Scoop into a bowl and put in the refrigerator.

2. In the empty mixer bowl (no need to wash), add cream cheese, and beat until smooth. Continue mixing and add remaining powdered sugar and vanilla. Add crushed pineapple, a little at a time, while slowly mixing.

3. Stop mixing and gently fold in (with a spatula) the cold whipped cream. Fold together until just combined.

More Ideas •

Feel free to use fresh ripe pineapple in place of the canned pineapple. Cut pineapple into chunks and then blend in a food processor until pieces are about the size of a pea. You may need to taste and adjust the amount of sugar according to the sweetness of the fruit.

COCONUT CREAM PUDDING

Pictured on pages 17 and 25

Makes 3½ cups

Ingredients

3 Tbsp. plus 1 tsp. cornstarch

½ cup sugar

2 eggs

1 can coconut milk
(1¾ cups)

¾ cup milk

1 tsp. vanilla extract

½ tsp. coconut extract

½ cup sweetened
shredded coconut

Directions

1. In a small bowl, whisk together the cornstarch and sugar and set aside.

2. In another small bowl, add eggs and beat well with a fork.

3. In a medium saucepan, add coconut milk and milk. Cook over medium heat until warm and then add sugar/starch mixture. Whisk vigorously until the sugar and starch are dissolved. Remove the pan from the heat.

4. Scoop out about 1 cup of the hot milk mixture. Pour a couple tablespoons of the hot milk into the bowl with the eggs. Whisk together. Continue adding just a bit of the hot milk at a time, while mixing, until you have added enough that the eggs are warm, and you have added the full cup of hot milk. Now pour the warm egg/milk mixture into the pan of milk and whisk together well.

5. Return the pan to the heat and continue cooking while slowly whisking almost constantly. Bring mixture to a slow boil and boil (while whisking) about 1 minute. The mixture should now be thickened.

6. Remove the pan from the heat and whisk in vanilla and coconut extract. Then stir in shredded coconut.

7. Allow to cool a few minutes and then move to the fridge to continue to cool. Chill about 4 hours, or up to 3 days. To prevent a skin from forming on the surface of the pudding, lay a piece of plastic wrap directly on the surface of the pudding.

CHEESECAKE MOUSSE

Makes 3 cups

This light and fluffy cheesecake dessert is delicious on its own and is also an extremely versatile base recipe for countless flavor options.

Ingredients

²/₃ cup heavy cream

¾ cup powdered sugar,
divided

1 (8-oz.) block cream cheese

1 tsp. vanilla

1 tsp. fresh lemon zest
(optional)

2 Tbsp. milk

Directions

1. In the bowl of an electric mixer, beat the heavy cream until it begins to thicken. While mixing, slowly add ¼ cup powdered sugar. Continue to beat until mixture is thickened and holds a stiff peak. Do not overbeat or it will become overly thick and clumpy. Scoop into a bowl and put in the refrigerator.

2. In the empty mixer (no need to wash), add cream cheese and beat until smooth. Continue mixing and add remaining powdered sugar, vanilla, and lemon zest (if desired). Add milk and beat until well combined.

3. Stop mixing and gently fold in (with a spatula) the cold whipped cream. Fold together until just combined.

4. Use immediately, or cover and keep in the refrigerator up to 1 day.

ALTERNATE METHOD •

Creamy Whipped Cheesecake

Using the same ingredients listed above, minus the milk, this alternate mixing method produces a slightly thicker and creamier cheesecake. Both methods produce an equally delicious dessert, and in any recipe that calls for one method, you could use either one.

Start with the cream cheese in the mixer. Beat until smooth. Add all ¾ cup powdered sugar, vanilla, and lemon zest (if desired) and blend until fully incorporated and smooth. Add (cold) heavy cream and whip until smooth and increased in volume by almost double.

Use immediately, or cover and store in the refrigerator up to 1 day.

CHOCOLATE MOUSSE

Makes 8–9 servings

This classic dessert is delicious and elegant on its own, but it can also be dressed up as a beautiful layered dessert.

Ingredients

2 eggs

¼ cup sugar

1 cup heavy whipping cream
(or half-and-half) plus 1½ cups
heavy whipping cream

6 oz. semisweet chocolate,
or 4 oz. semisweet and 2 oz.
bittersweet for a darker
chocolate flavor

Directions

1. Beat eggs with an electric mixer on high about 3 minutes. Gradually beat in sugar.

2. Heat 1 cup whipping cream (or half-and-half) in a saucepan over medium heat, just until hot.

3. A little at a time, pour about ½ cup of the hot cream into the beaten eggs, stirring constantly. Then add the warm egg/cream mixture to the saucepan. Cook over low heat about 5 minutes, stirring constantly, until mixture thickens (do not boil).

4. Remove from heat and add chocolate. Stir until the chocolate is melted. Cover and refrigerate about 2 hours, stirring occasionally.

5. When the chocolate mixture has chilled, beat 1½ cups whipping cream in a chilled bowl with an electric mixer. Beat on medium-high until stiff. Fold chocolate mixture into whipping cream, just until combined.

6. Serve immediately or refrigerate up to 4 hours.

Store-Bought Swap •

Check your grocery store for chocolate mousse mixes (usually sold near boxed pudding mix).

CHOCOLATE PUDDING

Makes 2½ cups (about 4 servings)

You may be surprised how easy it is to make pudding from scratch. By putting in a bit more effort than making boxed mix pudding, you will be rewarded with a rich, flavorful, and creamy treat. This pudding is delicious on its own and is also wonderful in a wide variety of layered desserts.

Ingredients

⅓ cup sugar

2 Tbsp. plus 1 tsp. cornstarch

2 cups milk

3 oz. bittersweet chocolate
(about 60% cacao)

1 Tbsp. butter

1 tsp. vanilla extract

Directions

1. In a small bowl, whisk sugar and cornstarch and set aside.

2. In a medium saucepan, add milk and chocolate. Heat over medium-high heat, stirring occasionally, until the chocolate has melted.

3. Add sugar/starch mixture to heated milk/chocolate, whisking vigorously until fully incorporated.

4. Continue to cook, whisking often, until mixture thickens.

5. Bring to a boil, and boil 1 minute, whisking constantly.

6. Remove pan from heat and add butter and vanilla. Stir to fully combine.

7. Stir slowly an additional minute or so, to help pudding cool.

8. Can be enjoyed warm, if desired, or cool fully. To prevent a skin from forming on the surface of the pudding, lay a piece of plastic wrap directly on the surface of the pudding. Move to the refrigerator to cool completely (about 2 hours). Store up to 2 days.

Store-Bought Swap • • • • • • • • • • • • • • • • • • •

For any recipe that calls for chocolate pudding, you could use store-bought prepared pudding or a pudding mix.

PEANUT BUTTER MOUSSE

Pictured on pages 34 and 62

Makes 3½ cups

Ingredients

¾ cup heavy cream

1½ cups powdered sugar,
divided

4 oz. cream cheese
(½ block)

½ cup natural peanut butter*
(no sugar added)

2 Tbsp. milk
(any fat content)

½ tsp. vanilla

*If you do not have natural peanut butter,
you will likely need to reduce the amount
of added sugar.

Directions

1. In the bowl of an eclectic mixer, beat heavy cream until it begins to thicken. Add ¼ cup powdered sugar, while mixing, and continue to beat until cream is thick and holds a stiff peak. Scoop whipped cream into a bowl and put in the refrigerator.

2. In your empty mixing bowl (no need to wash), add cream cheese and blend until smooth. Add peanut butter and blend until fully incorporated. Slowly add remaining 1¼ cups powdered sugar. Add milk and vanilla. Beat until all ingredients are fully incorporated. Fold in whipped cream, using a spatula.

3. Divide mixture into serving dishes or refrigerate until ready to use.

MANGO PUREE

Pictured on page 53

Makes ⅔ cup

Ingredients

1 cup fresh or frozen
mango chunks

1 Tbsp. fresh lemon juice

1 Tbsp. sugar

Directions

1. If using frozen mango, allow to thaw at room temperature a bit before blending. Blend mango pieces in a blender or food processor until smooth.

2. Add lemon juice and sugar and blend until fully incorporated. Taste and adjust sugar as needed.

3. If desired, pour the mango puree through a fine strainer to create a perfectly smooth puree. Keep puree in the refrigerator until ready to use.

CREAMY NO-BAKE CHEESECAKE

Makes 3½ cups

This luscious no-bake cheesecake has been a favorite in our family as long as I can remember. I used to make this as a teenager, when my boyfriend (now husband) would come over for dinner. It has always been a favorite of his, and it still is twenty years later.

Ingredients

Graham Cracker Crumble
(see page 84)

12 oz. cream cheese
(1½ blocks)

1 (14-oz.) can sweetened
condensed milk

¼ cup fresh lemon juice

1 tsp. vanilla

topping of choice
(optional)

Directions

1. Prepare crumble. (For a traditional crust see "more ideas" below.)

2. Using an electric mixer, beat the cream cheese until fully smooth. While still mixing, slowly pour in the condensed milk. Blend until well incorporated.

3. Continue mixing and add the lemon juice and vanilla.

4. Beat until all the ingredients are well combined.

5. Pour onto crumble and chill at least 3 hours. The cheesecake can be made up to 2 days in advance and kept (covered) in the refrigerator.

6. Top cheesecake with fresh fruit, fruit sauce (page 122), canned pie filling, or chocolate ganache (page 128), or enjoy plain.

More Ideas

You can make the classic version of this dessert by making one large pie. Follow the recipe for graham cracker crumble on page 84 but increase the sugar from 1 tablespoon to 2 tablespoons. Then, instead of spreading the crumbs onto a baking sheet, press crumbs into a standard (9-inch) pie plate. Bake crust for 10 minutes (or until light golden brown) in a 350°F oven. Allow crust to cool before adding cheesecake filling.

VANILLA PANNA COTTA

Makes 6–8 servings, or 3 cups

Panna cotta, Italian for "cooked cream" is a creamy and delicious dessert with endless flavor options. If you've never had panna cotta, it could be described as a cross between pudding and Jell-O.

Ingredients

1 cup milk
(any fat content), divided

2 tsp. powdered gelatin

2 cups heavy cream

3 Tbsp. sugar

1 tsp. vanilla extract

Directions

1. Pour about ½ cup of milk into a small bowl, and then add remaining milk to a medium saucepan. Sprinkle the gelatin in the small bowl of milk and set aside (leave undisturbed 5–10 minutes).

2. Add cream to the saucepan and heat the milk and cream until hot but not boiling. Add the sugar and whisk until fully dissolved.

3. Remove pan from the heat and add the bowl of milk and gelatin. Whisk mixture in pan until the gelatin has fully dissolved, 1–2 minutes.

4. Add vanilla.

5. Pour panna cotta mixture into the dishes of your choice. Move dishes to the refrigerator and allow to chill 3–4 hours. The panna cotta can be kept (covered) in the refrigerator up to 2 days.

CHOCOLATE PANNA COTTA

Using the same recipe as listed above, once you have heated the milk/cream mixture, remove pan from heat and add 4 ounces chopped semisweet chocolate (it is important that the chocolate has been chopped into small pieces so it will melt quickly). Allow the chocolate to sit in the hot cream at least 1 minute and then whisk well to fully combine. Once the chocolate is incorporated, add the bowl of gelatin and milk and whisk until the gelatin is fully dissolved, 1–2 minutes. Pour into dessert dishes and refrigerate as directed above.

RASPBERRY & BLACKBERRY CHEESECAKE MOUSSES

Pictured on page 73

Makes 6 servings

Ingredients

⅔ cup heavy cream

¾ cup powdered sugar, divided

1 (8-oz.) block cream cheese

1 tsp. vanilla

¼ cup raspberry puree, made from ½-⅔ cup fresh or frozen raspberries

¼ cup blackberry puree, made from ½-⅔ cup fresh or frozen blackberries

2 Tbsp. raspberry jam, or 1 Tbsp. raspberry jam and 1 Tbsp. blackberry jam

Directions

1. In the bowl of an electric mixer, beat the heavy cream until it begins to thicken. While mixing, slowly add ¼ cup powdered sugar. Continue to beat until mixture is thickened and holds a stiff peak. Do not overbeat or it will become overly thick and clumpy. Scoop the whipped cream into 2 medium bowls, with about half of the whipped cream in each, and put the bowls in the refrigerator.

2. In the empty mixer (no need to wash), add cream cheese and beat until smooth. Continue mixing and add remaining powdered sugar and vanilla. Stop mixing and do your best to divide the mixture in half, leaving half in the mixing bowl and putting half aside in another bowl.

3. Add the raspberry puree and 1 tablespoon jam to the cream cheese in the mixing bowl. Blend until smooth. Use a spatula to fold in one of the bowls of whipped cream. Once blended, scoop all of the raspberry cheesecake mixture into a bowl and set in the refrigerator.

4. Repeat similar process for blackberry. Take the remaining small bowl of blended cream cheese, add it to the mixer, and blend in the blackberry puree and 1 tablespoon jam. Fold in the remaining bowl of whipped cream until fully incorporated. Once blended, scoop all of the blackberry cheesecake mixture into a bowl and set in the refrigerator. Chill at least 15 minutes or up to 2 hours before serving.

KEY LIME CHEESECAKE

Pictured on pages 46 and 53

Makes 3 cups

Ingredients

1 (8-oz.) block
cream cheese

1 (14-oz.) can sweetened
condensed milk

¼ cup fresh lime juice
(you'll need 3–4 limes
on average),
or key lime juice

1 tsp. lime zest
finely chopped

3 Tbsp. Greek yogurt
(any fat content),
or sour cream

1 tsp. vanilla

Directions

1. In the bowl of an electric mixer, beat cream cheese until smooth.

2. Slowly pour in sweetened condensed milk while mixing. Mix until fully incorporated and smooth.

3. Add lime juice and zest and continue to blend. Add yogurt (or sour cream) and vanilla, and mix until all ingredients are well incorporated.

4. Pour into desired containers and chill at least 3 hours.

VANILLA PASTRY CREAM

Makes 3½ cups

This rich and creamy custard is a versatile dessert. Pastry cream is similar to vanilla pudding and can be used interchangeably.

Ingredients

2 eggs

⅔ cup sugar

¼ cup cornstarch

½ tsp. salt

3 cups milk

2 Tbsp. butter

1 Tbsp. vanilla extract,
or 2 tsp. vanilla extract
and 1 tsp. vanilla
bean paste

Directions

1. In a medium bowl, beat eggs with a fork to combine. Set aside.

2. In a medium saucepan, whisk together sugar, cornstarch, and salt. Gradually pour in milk while whisking. Cook over medium heat, stirring almost constantly until the mixture thickens and boils. Continue to cook and stir 1 minute. Remove pan from the heat.

3. Pour several tablespoons of the hot mixture into the bowl with the eggs and immediately stir well. Continue to add a few more tablespoons of hot milk mixture, and stir with the eggs until the eggs are warm. Pour the warmed egg mixture into the pan with the rest of the hot milk mixture. Return to a slow boil and cook 1 minute, stirring constantly.

4. Remove pan from heat and stir in butter and vanilla. Set aside to cool slightly. When the pan has cooled a bit, place in the refrigerator to fully cool (about 3 hours). If desired, lay a piece of plastic wrap directly on the surface of the pastry cream to prevent a skin from forming.

Store-Bought Swap •

For any recipe that calls for this vanilla pastry cream, you could use prepared vanilla pudding or a vanilla pudding mix.

PUMPKIN MOUSSE

Pictured on page 69

Makes 4½ cups

Ingredients

1¼ cups heavy cream

1 cup powdered sugar,
divided

1 (8-oz.) block cream cheese

1 cup pumpkin puree (canned)

1 tsp. cinnamon

¼ tsp. cloves

¼ tsp. nutmeg

1 tsp. vanilla

1 Tbsp. milk
or cream

Directions

1. In the bowl of an electric mixer, whip heavy cream until it begins to thicken. While mixing, slowly add ¼ cup powdered sugar. Continue to whip until the cream is thick and holds its shape. Scoop whipped cream into a bowl and place in the refrigerator.

2. In the empty mixer (no need to wash), add cream cheese and beat until smooth. Add pumpkin puree and blend until incorporated. Add remaining powdered sugar, cinnamon, cloves, and nutmeg. Continue blending and add vanilla and milk (or cream). Continue mixing until all ingredients are well blended.

3. Stop mixer and then use a spatula to fold the whipped cream (from the fridge) into the pumpkin mixture. Blend gently just until combined.

4. Use immediately or keep (covered) in the refrigerator up to 1 full day.

Sauces & Toppings

CARAMEL SAUCE

Makes 1 cup

I've been intimidated by the idea of making homemade caramel for quite a while, but I love it so much I had to just keep trying to figure it out! Although you do need to keep a close watch on the pan, this recipe is quite easy, and you'll be so pleased with the delicious caramel sauce it creates!

Ingredients

½ cup heavy cream

1 cup sugar

1 Tbsp. corn syrup

¼ cup water

3 Tbsp. butter

¾ tsp. salt
(such as good-quality sea salt)

1 tsp. vanilla extract

Directions

1. Warm the heavy cream in a bowl in the microwave and then set aside.

2. In a large saucepan, add the sugar, corn syrup, and water. Stir gently to incorporate the ingredients.

3. Cook over medium to medium-high heat, stirring gently, until the sugar dissolves and the mixture is bubbling.

4. Stop stirring and allow the mixture to boil undisturbed until it begins to darken in color. You want the mixture to reach a honey color, but no darker. The syrup will change from light in color to dark very quickly, so it's important to watch closely and remove the pan from the heat as soon as it's a light-medium honey color.

5. Once removed from heat, carefully and slowly pour in the warm heavy cream (the mixture will hiss and bubble). Stir to fully incorporate the cream.

6. Add butter and salt and stir to combine. Add vanilla.

7. Allow sauce to cool a bit and then pour into a jar. Store the caramel in the refrigerator, up to 1 month.

8. Warm the sauce in the microwave before use, as desired.

Store-Bought Swap ·

Any recipe that calls for caramel sauce, you can swap with a store-bought caramel sauce. Look for good-quality, thick caramel sauce made with real cream and sugar.

CHOCOLATE FUDGE SAUCE

Makes 1 cup

You'll never buy hot fudge sauce again once you realize how easy and delicious this homemade sauce is! This decadent sauce is wonderful for dipping fresh fruit, beautiful as a garnish, and delicious as an ice cream topping.

Ingredients

⅓ cup heavy cream

¼ cup corn syrup

3 Tbsp. brown sugar

2 Tbsp. unsweetened cocoa powder

3 oz. semisweet chocolate

1 Tbsp. butter

1 tsp. vanilla extract

Directions

1. Add cream, corn syrup, brown sugar, cocoa powder, and chocolate to a medium saucepan.

2. Heat over medium heat, stirring occasionally, until the chocolate is melted.

3. Bring mixture to a boil, while continuing to stir occasionally.

4. Cook at a low boil about 5 minutes, while stirring slowly.

5. Remove pan from heat and add the butter and vanilla. Stir to combine.

6. Allow to cool a few minutes and then pour into a heat-safe jar to continue to cool.

7. Use at once, or store in the refrigerator (in a covered jar) up to 2 weeks. Reheat before use.

Store-Bought Swap •

For recipes that call for this chocolate fudge sauce, you could use a store-bought hot fudge sauce or thick chocolate sauce. Look for a good-quality sauce made with real sugar, cream, and cocoa.

HOMEMADE FRUIT SAUCE

Makes 2 cups

Enjoy the bounty of spring and summer with this delicious fruit sauce. Use the fruit of your choice—such as berries, cherries, or peaches—to create a topping for ice cream, cheesecake, or pancakes.

Ingredients

½ cup water

2 Tbsp. fresh lemon juice

½ cup sugar

1 Tbsp. cornstarch

2 cups fresh or frozen
fruit of choice*
(blueberries shown)

*Depending on the ripeness of the fruit, you may need to adjust the amount of sugar.

Directions

1. In a medium saucepan, add water and lemon juice and warm over medium heat.

2. In a small bowl, stir together the sugar and cornstarch with a whisk. Then add the sugar and starch to the warm pan of liquid and stir (with a whisk) to combine.

3. Add fruit and continue to cook, while stirring gently, until the sauce thickens.

4. Remove pan from heat and allow sauce to cool. Store the sauce (in a jar or sealed container) in the refrigerator, up to 1 week.

Store-Bought Swap ·

If desired, you can swap this homemade sauce for canned pie filling.

LEMON CURD

Makes 1 cup

Despite the unusual name, lemon curd is an incredibly delicious and versatile ingredient. Enjoy it on pancakes, waffles, or toast, or add to cream cheese, whipped cream, or yogurt.

Ingredients

¼ cup fresh lemon juice
(usually requires 1–2 lemons)

2 tsp. finely grated
lemon zest

⅓ cup sugar

4 egg yolks

3 Tbsp. butter

Directions

1. Combine all ingredients in the top of a double boiler (or in a metal bowl over a pot of simmering water).

2. Heat, while stirring (with a whisk), until the mixture thickens.

3. The lemon curd is done when it's thick enough to coat the back of a spoon.

4. Remove from heat, cover, and refrigerate until cool. If desired, pour the lemon curd through a fine strainer before refrigerating.

5. Store the lemon curd in the refrigerator up to 2 weeks.

Store-Bought Swap • • • • • • • • • • • • • • • •

Look for lemon curd where jams and jellies are sold.

WHIPPED CREAM

Makes 2¾ cups

Homemade whipped cream is easy to make, and it is such an amazingly delicious dessert element and garnish.

Ingredients

> 1 cup heavy cream
>
> ¼ cup powdered sugar
>
> ½ tsp. vanilla extract

Store-Bought Swap

In recipes where the whipped cream is used mostly as a garnish, feel free to use canned whipped cream or nondairy whipped topping (such as Cool Whip). In recipes where the whipped cream is a layering component, you can use nondairy whipped topping.

Directions

1. Chill the bowl and beater (whisk attachment) of your electric mixer by placing them in the freezer about 5 minutes. This will help your cream whip up faster and fuller.

2. When the bowl has chilled, pour cream into bowl and begin whipping on medium-high speed.

3. When the cream is beginning to thicken, slowly add the powdered sugar, while continuing to beat.

4. Add vanilla, while mixing.

5. The whipped cream is done when it has more than doubled in volume and, when you stop the mixer and lift up the whisk, the cream stays in place.

6. Do not overmix or the cream will become too stiff, will become clumpy, and will begin to turn into butter.

7. Use whipped cream immediately, or keep in the refrigerator up to 4 hours.

STABILIZED WHIPPED CREAM ·

If you need to make the whipped cream a day ahead of serving, or if you will be serving your dessert in extra-warm weather, you may want to make stabilized whipped cream. There is no difference in taste or texture, but the addition of gelatin will help the whipped cream keep its shape a full day or more. To make stabilized whipped cream, you'll need the ingredients listed above, plus ½ teaspoon powdered gelatin (sold near Jell-O) and 2 tablespoons warm water. Put the warm water in a small bowl and sprinkle the gelatin over the water. Allow the gelatin to sit about 5 minutes and then stir to dissolve the gelatin in the water. Follow the directions listed above, and after the cream has begun to thicken and you have added the powdered sugar, slowly pour in the (now cool) dissolved gelatin and water. Add vanilla and continue to whip, as directed above.

CHOCOLATE GANACHE

Pictured on page 37

Makes ¾ cup

Ingredients

4 oz. heavy cream

4 oz. semisweet chocolate,
chopped

Directions

1. Pour cream into a small saucepan. Heat the cream until hot but not boiling. Remove pan from heat and add chopped chocolate (no need to stir). Allow chocolate to melt on its own in the hot cream (a few minutes). Then stir well to combine.

2. Place the pan in the refrigerator and allow the sauce to thicken. Check on the ganache after 15 minutes and then again every 15 minutes or so until it's reached the desired thickness. The ganache will continue to thicken as it cools and, after a couple hours, will be about the consistency of fudge. The sauce can be reheated (to thin).

WHIPPED LEMON CREAM

Pictured on page 49

Makes 2½ cups

Ingredients

4 oz. cream cheese
(½ block)

1 cup heavy cream

½ cup powdered sugar

2 Tbsp. Lemon Curd
(see page 125),
or use store-bought

½ tsp. vanilla extract

Directions

1. In the bowl of an electric mixer, beat cream cheese until smooth. Add heavy cream slowly, while mixing. When the cream begins to thicken, slowly add powdered sugar and then lemon curd and vanilla. Continue to beat until all ingredients are well incorporated and the mixture is light and fluffy.

2. Use immediately, or store in the refrigerator up to 2 hours.

TIPS FOR LARGE TRIFLES

Many of the layered desserts in this book work equally well as a large trifle. In most cases you will need to double the ingredients listed in the original recipes. For easy reference, here are recipes that work especially well as a large trifle. I've also noted the changes needed in order to fill (or mostly fill) a large trifle dish.

Banana Caramel Cream Dessert (page 12): Double the whipped cream and bananas.

Brownie Bottom Coconut Cream Dessert (page 16): Make a double batch of whipped cream and use it as a layer in the dessert as well as garnish. Also, increase the amount of toasted coconut and layer it in the dessert as well.

Brownie Strawberry Shortcake (pictured, recipe on page 19): Double the whipped cream and strawberries.

Caramel Brownie Trifle (page 23): Double the chocolate pudding and whipped cream, and use 4 candy bars.

Chocolate-Covered Banana Dessert (page 27): Make a double batch of whipped cream and use it as a layer in the dessert, in addition to a garnish. Double the chocolate pudding and the bananas.

Fresh Fruit Cheesecake Mousse (page 43): Double the cheesecake mousse, and increase the amount of fruit.

Lemon Blueberry Trifle (page 48): Double the whipped lemon cream and the blueberries.

Peach Raspberry Almond Trifle (page 59): Double the creamy whipped cheesecake, and increase the amount of fruit.

Pumpkin Spice Cake Trifle (page 71): Double the creamy whipped cheesecake.

Summer Berry Trifle (page 79): Increase the amount of fruit.

RESOURCES

Listed below are the sources to each of the glasses and jars shown in this book. Although you may not be able to find all of the exact same jars, each of the stores and websites listed are great places to find several different glasses and dishes that work beautifully for layered desserts. Some dishes are sold specifically as individual trifle dishes (such as number 15 on the next page), but in general any small juice glass works nicely. I prefer glasses that hold four to ten ounces.

1. World Market (worldmarket.com)

2. Small juice glass, found at my local grocery store

3. Walmart, 9-oz. juice glass, sold in a pack of 4

4. Crate and Barrel (crateandbarrel.com)

5. Libbey brand, 4.75-oz., available from webstaurantstore.com

6. World Market (worldmarket.com)

7. Libbey brand, available from Target, Pier 1 Imports, and Bed Bath & Beyond

8. Libbey brand, available from Pier 1 Imports and Bed Bath & Beyond

9. Almost identical to number 8, but another brand, found at Home Goods

10. IKEA

11. Found at my local thrift store

12. Found at my local thrift store

13. World Market (worldmarket.com)

14. Found at a discount home décor store (Tuesday Morning)

15. Walmart (similar available from Target)

16. Walmart, 8-oz. widemouthed canning jar (also found at my local grocery store)

17. Walmart, 8-oz. regular-mouthed canning jar (also found at my local grocery store)

18. Weck brand, 5.4-oz., available at Crate and Barrel (crateandbarrel.com) and weckjars.com

Note: Jar numbers 16–18 are sold with lids, making them great options for transporting to picnics and parties.

ADDITIONAL RESOURCES

DISPOSABLE OPTIONS *(SHOWN RIGHT)*

- Aqua stripe, pastel polka-dot, and pink-and-white polka-dot paper ice cream bowls (Sambellina brand), available from Shop Sweet Lulu (shopsweetlulu.com)

- Smaller white paper ice cream bowls, available from Shop Sweet Lulu (shopsweetlulu.com) and the TomKat Studio (shoptomkat.com)

- Yellow polka-dot and blue polka-dot cupcake cups/snack cups, available from the TomKat Studio (shoptomkat.com) and Shop Sweet Lulu (shopsweetlulu.com)

- Small wooden spoons

    Plain: Available from Garnish (thinkgarnish.com), the TomKat Studio (shoptomkat.com) and Shop Sweet Lulu (shopsweetlulu.com)

    Patterned: Available from Shop Sweet Lulu (shopsweetlulu.com)

- Small clear plastic cups (5 oz.), available from webstaurantstore.com

- Clear plastic wine glass, available from Dollar Tree (dollartree.com)

- Cake stand, available from Pier 1 Imports

ADDITIONAL SUPPLIES SHOWN IN THE BOOK

- Small metal spoons, available from World Market (worldmarket.com) and Crate and Barrel (crateandbarrel.com)

- Large trifle dish (pictured on page 129), available from Walmart. Similar dishes available at most kitchen or home goods stores.

- Piping bags (also called pastry bags) and large piping tips, available from Michaels, Jo-Ann, Hobby Lobby, and sweetbakingsupply.com

SPECIAL DIETS

The beauty of making desserts from scratch is you have control over every ingredient used. This allows you to make adjustments to fit your needs. When making food for people with special diets, check the labels of each ingredient used to make sure it fits their needs. The following lists are suggestions only. You may still need to make additional adjustments, depending on the products available in your area.

MOST EASILY ADAPTABLE TO **GLUTEN-FREE**

Banana Caramel Cream Dessert (page 12): Replace graham cracker crumble with sugared nuts (page 92) or toasted coconut.

Chocolate Coconut Layered Pudding (page 24)

Chocolate-Covered Banana Dessert (page 27): Omit brownies.

Chocolate Mousse (page 102)

Fresh Fruit Cheesecake Mousse (page 43)

Mango Lime Coconut Cheesecake (page 52): Replace coconut graham cracker crumble with toasted coconut.

Peach Raspberry Almond Trifle (page 59): Omit sponge cake.

Peaches & Cream (page 60)

Piña Colada Cheesecake Mousse (page 64): Replace coconut graham cracker crumble with toasted coconut.

Pumpkin Mousse Parfait (page 68): Replace cinnamon nut crumble with sugared nuts (page 92) or toasted nuts of your choice.

Raspberry Blackberry Cheesecake Mousse (page 72)

Strawberries on a Chocolate Cloud (page 75)

Strawberry Cheesecake Mousse (page 76)

Vanilla Panna Cotta (page 111)

MOST EASILY ADAPTABLE TO **SUGAR-FREE**

For the following recipes, omit the sugar listed and replace with a sugar substitute (such as Splenda). Start with ½ of the listed measurement and then taste and adjust as needed. Another alternative for these recipes would be to replace the sugar and heavy cream listed with sugar-free whipped topping (such as sugar-free Cool Whip).

Fresh Fruit Cheesecake Mousse (page 43)

Peaches & Cream (page 60)

Raspberry Blackberry Cheesecake Mousse (page 72)

Strawberry Cheesecake Mousse (page 76)

MOST EASILY ADAPTABLE TO **EGG-FREE**

Apple Crisp (page 11)

Banana Split Cheesecake (page 15)

Caramel Apple Cheesecake (page 20)

Chocolate-Covered Banana Dessert (page 27): Replace brownies with chocolate cookie crumble (page 83).

Chocolate Mint Crunch (page 31)

Chocolate Peanut Butter Trifle (page 35): Replace brownies with chocolate cookie crumble (page 83).

Chocolate Raspberry Cheesecake (page 36)

Cookies & Cream Cheesecake (page 39)

Creamy No-Bake Cheesecake with Blueberry Sauce (page 40)

Fresh Fruit Cheesecake Mousse (page 43)

Fried Ice Cream Cheesecake (page 44)

Key lime Coconut Cheesecake (page 47)

Mango Lime Coconut Cheesecake (page 52)

Orange Vanilla Panna Cotta (page 56)

Peaches & Cream (page 60)

Peanut Butter Mousse with Chocolate Cookie Crumble (page 63)

Piña Colada Cheesecake Mousse (page 64)

Pumpkin Mousse Parfait (page 68)

Raspberry Blackberry Cheesecake Mousse (page 72)

Strawberry Cheesecake Mousse (page 76)

INDEX

ACKNOWLEDGMENTS

I thank God for his unending grace, patience, and love, and I aim to honor him in all I do. I am so thankful to God for leading me toward a career where I am able to use the creativity he's gifted me with. And I'm especially grateful for all the people the Lord has brought into my life to encourage me along the way.

Eternal thanks to my husband, James. Without your unending support, encouragement, and patience, I would not be the person I am today, and I would not have been able to see so many of my dreams come true. You are the most amazing husband and father! And you're a pretty great editor, taste tester, sous-chef, and dishwasher too. Thank you for all you do!

For your unending encouragement and support, thank you to my parents, Bud and Laura Mailhot; my sisters, Lacie Robertson and Joy Adams; my in-laws, Gary and Lorrie Albin; and my sister-in-law, Rebecca Albin.

Special thanks to friends who have encouraged me, supported me, and cheered me on for many years.

These are friends who gladly sampled my "experiments," oohed and ahhed over my creations, and spoke words of encouragement into my life, often when it was more needed than they knew:

Cecilia Midgette, Amy Middleton, Heather Serpa, Sharnel Dollar, Shelly Lange, Sharon Flath, Pam Smith, Tara Loorz, Jeanna Robertson, Carolyn Holcomb, Dawn Liberti, Maryann Rollins, Kim Stoegbauer, and Callye Alvarado.

A huge thank you to my photographer, Gene Chutka. Without your patience, attention to detail, and hard work, this book would have likely never come together.

Thank you to each of the readers of my blog, GloriousTreats.com, who have left sweet and encouraging comments on the various recipes, parties, and projects I have posted over the past few years. Every positive word has meant the world to me. Thank you!

ABOUT THE AUTHOR

Glory Albin is the author of the popular dessert and entertaining blog GloriousTreats.com. Glory's clean, elegant design style and creative ideas have drawn millions of readers to her site. Glory's work has been featured on *The Martha Stewart Show*, MarthaStewart.com, HGTV.com, *The Oprah Blog*, BonAppétit.com, *Parenting* magazine, *Woman's World* magazine, and countless other food, style, and craft websites. Glory lives in beautiful Northern California with her husband and two young daughters.

Praise for *Glorious* Layered Desserts

"An utterly beautiful and modern take on the traditional trifle, Glory's book is bound to inspire. Filled with mouthwatering recipes and gorgeous photographs, it's a must-have for any dessert lover."

—Marian Poirier, Sweetopia (sweetopia.net)

"From Brownie Strawberry Shortcake to Pumpkin Caramel Banana Trifle, each one of Glory Albin's creations is, well, glorious. *Glorious Layered Desserts* takes layered treats beyond your grandmother's trifle bowl . . . with recipes for creating impressive individual desserts for any occasion."

—Bridget Edwards, Bake at 350 (bakeat350.blogspot.com), author of
Decorating Cookies: 60+ Designs for Holidays, Celebrations & Everyday

"This gorgeous book is filled with amazing recipes for creating delicious layered desserts. Glory Albin teaches us how to prepare and display treats perfectly for any holiday or occasion."

—Kim Stoegbauer, the TomKat Studio (thetomkatstudio.com)

"*Glorious Layered Desserts* celebrates your favorite flavors lovingly layered in miniature form. From cakes and crumbles to fillings and sauces, Glory's recipes are quick and customizable, making it easy for you to create beautiful desserts."

—Angie Dudley, Bakerella (bakerella.com), author of *Cake Pops:
Tips, Tricks, and Recipes for More Than 40 Irresistible Mini Treats*